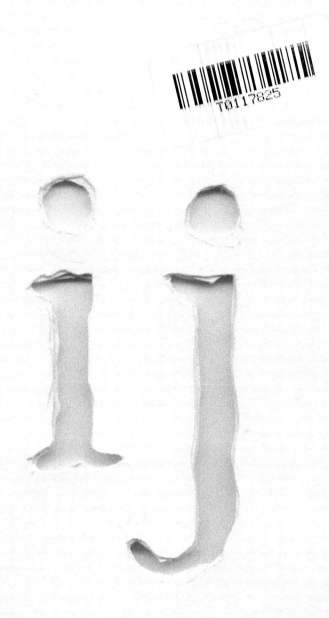

Bone Light

poems

Orlando White

RED HEN PRESS | Los Angeles, California

Bone Light
Copyright © 2009 by Orlando White

ISBN: 978-1-59709-135-0
Library of Congress Catalog Card Number: 2008941917

Endpaper images by Donna Charging

Layout assistance by Sydney Nichols

The California Arts Council and the National Endowment for the Arts partially support Red Hen Press.

Published by Red Hen Press
www.redhen.org

First Edition

ACKNOWLEDGEMENTS

Grateful acknowledgement is made to the editors of the following publications in which these poems, sometimes in earlier versions, first appeared:

Exittheapple: "Bone Milk"; *In Posse Review*: "Meditation"; *Oregon Literary Review*: "Quietus"; *Ploughshares*: "Sentence"; *Red Ink Magazine*: "Bone Light"; The Institute of American Indian Arts Student Anthologies: *Bone Light*: "On the Zero's Eye" and "Square Lips"; *Neon and Chlorophyll*: "Skin of a Letter," "Light Bulb Eye," "Dissolve," "Bleach Ink," "i Without j," "From Skin to Bone," and "To See Letters"; *Fish Head Soup*: "Imperative" and "Discourse"; & *Scrimshaw*: "Skeleton," "Dot Fly," "Circle Shape," and "Writ"; *To Topos*: "Ars Poetica," "i-j," and "Ats'íísts'in"; *26 Magazine*: "Open Dark," "Fill in the Blank," "Images of Myself," "The i is a Cricket," "Lower Case i and j," and "Blank Circle"; and *Ur Vox*: "Blank Skull," "Human Clock," and "i Next to j."

Thanks to my mother, Mae Phyllis White, for her love and patience; to my brothers and sister: Ty, Gabrial, and Sandie, who are the best; to my grandpa, Bert Whitehair Youngboy, for his prayers; my family and relatives, who always nourish me; to my friends and teachers: Sherwin Bitsui, Jennifer Foerster, Santee Frazier, Melanie Cesspooch, Richard Castaneda, DG Nanouk Okpik, Britta Andersson, Sara Ortiz, Allison Adelle Hedge Coke, Elizabeth Robinson, Evelina Zuni Lucero, Arthur Sze, and Jon Davis, for their undying support and encouragement; to the Institute of American Indian Arts, for providing a space for me to write and express; and finally to Layli Long Soldier and Chance Ohitika Alexie White, who continuously balance my life.

For Mae Phyllis White & Bert Whitehair Youngboy

Contents

Bone Light

To See Letters

Everything I write requires this: Alphabet.

It was a notion I did not know when I was six years old. In kindergarten I was more interested in the image of a letter on a flash card. I noticed its shape distinguishing itself from its background. Then, with my eyes I tore the O in half. In that moment I felt language separate from its form.

I recall my mother playing a word puzzle. She'd circle a line of letters amongst many other letters scattered on the page. She treated each word carefully never touching the pen to the letters. Then, she would give me the pen. I would circle random letters. She'd smile and give me a hug.

My mother once told me that my step-dad found a picture of my real father. He ripped it up. To this day, I still do not know who my father is.

I always called my step-dad, David. And he called me by my middle name, Orson. To him it was better than looking at me and calling me "son." I am still ashamed of my middle name.

He tried to teach me how to spell.

I showed him homework from my first grade class. It was a list of words assigned for me to spell. He looked at me as he was sharpening a pencil with his knife. I remember the way he forced my hand to write. How the pencil stabbed each letter, the lead smearing. I imagined each word bruising as I stared at them.

The words reminded me of the word puzzle.

But without images it meant nothing at all.

He said, "Spell them out."
I could not. "Then sound them out first!"

I recall a day, like many other days in grammar school, when an older boy made fun of me because I could not speak proper English. I always mispronounced words, and I would wonder how to spell them.

I still could not move the pencil in my hand. I saw the letters lined up on paper, but I wanted to circle them.

He shouted out, "Spell them out you little fucker! I am going to hit you if you don't."

I remember the shape of his fist.

No one was around, not even my mother. It was as close to intimacy as I got with my step-dad. I did not say anything to anyone. He bought me toys as an act of contrition. I forgave him.

When David hit me in the head, I saw stars in the shape of the Alphabet. Years later, my fascination for letters resulted in poems.

Sentence

Look:

paper screen

blank;

the color white,

a zero,

hollow light bulb,

the O   not yet typed.

This means

no imagination
without
its *imagery*.

Letters   can appear

as bones

(Do not forget the image)

if you   write with   calcium.

Because a subject

can be half a skeleton,

the verb, the other half

and the skull,

a period.

The i is a Cricket

The book is open.

Can you hear

and see

the cricket?

Listen.

It sounds as if

someone is rubbing

the bristles

of two combs together.

Look closer.

Legs are struggling

like an upside down fly,

like a blinking eyelash.

Touch it.

And you will feel

its tiny hairs.

There is a letter

on the page

that has bent legs.

Before you close

the book

let it leap off the paper.

Bone Light

1.

Soak wash cloth
in bleach.

Put it   on face.

2.

Open the book
of a mouth.

Read one page.

Pull on
its black teeth

and remove
each period
with a fingernail.

3.

Empty   page:

pour letters
into a hollow skull.

Do not refill the page.

4.

Look inside
  the O
and blink once.

Stare at a zero
and you will see _____.

5.

Turn a question
mark clockwise
into
the socket:

          it will turn on.

Push the i:

          its head
          will not move.

6.

Let go of the skin
and watch it
fall into   a sink.

Fill in the Blank

1.

Ink: proof of existence.

2.

Bones

shattered

          on   black:

subject   and   verb.

3.

If you

break a skeleton

in half;

put   it back

together:

a complete   thought.

4.

Use   a pen

to puncture

a skull;

seeps   into comma.

5.

The sentence,

a structure

of   two parts.

6.

Punctuation: use it

to connect   the bones.

Ats'iists'in

Below the skull there is part of a letter

shaped like a bone. But the skull is not a skull;

it is a black dot with white teeth. And the piece

of the letter under it is not really a bone,

rather a dark spine. This is not the end of language.

When it was alive it had a ribcage;

each rib taken out by small pincers

the way strands of eyelash are removed

from eyelids. And the dot used to have eyes—

white like two grains of salt. But they were dissolved

by two drops of ink. The way a letter fades

on the page after many years of reading

or how it soaks into a fingerprint and forgets itself.

The way a word tries to breathe inside

a closed book; the way a letter shivers when

a page is turned. Because underneath sound

there is thought. Language, a complete structure

within the white coffin of paper. If you shake it

and listen, it will move, rattle like bones on the page.

Light Bulb Eye

From   dark

      to   paper

form   exists;

   text stencil   of thought,

absorbs   into.

Ink   pales

        as it

        dilutes.

Don't be afraid

          to see   the color _____.

Light

      shaped

      by circle,

alphabet

       on   fingertip:

   peel off   the O

   put on   eye,

         let it   blink.

Dissolve

The eye touches   chlorine surface.

   An O bends its knees,

                crawls acrosspaper.

     Its tail   a vital sign.

        The light bulb   begins to ripple.

     Ringing   inside a circle.

Bleach   discoloring.

     White heat   under   skin.

       The eye   begins to   vibrate.

     Eyelashes   quiver.

Letters fold   between   breaths.

     In the center   of a zero,   an echo.

Circle Shape

Trace a circle on top of another. Both are alike but do not mean the same thing.

Divide zero by zero: both are not something on either side of its given place.

Listen to the clock without numbers, the sound of something not written on.

Write the letter O; see the straight-line curve one end into the other.

Use the color _____ to fill in the black dot at the end of a thought.

Without empty form there would be no given fixed point: the center of zero.

The letter L bends white on paper. But the letter O lends itself to be bent by space.

The outline of a zero should roll off the paper after it is written.

The center of black: blank shaped like a circle. Do not think outside of this.

Open Dark

Skull   rolls

across

      black paper;

lower jaw   bone

        falls off.

Pick it   up.

Attach   to upper jaw:

     a half

        written   O.

Shake   the dark

page:

     no   words.

Use   white

     ink   to write;

     draw

an outline

     of   a letter

     that is   a circle

and watch

        its mouth   not close.

Bleach Ink

Erase   numbers

      from   clock.

Shake   the O

   until   white

appears;

      place over   skull.

You   are not

    blank

    or   white

but   a letter

shaped

    in   a black suit

    or black dress;

with   a face

that is   a dot

    of a   zero.

Human Clock

1.

Inside a mouth of
twelve fingers, the left
hand moves each
minute from its place,

slipping itself into
a glove shaped like
the circle.

2.

A tongue licks
numbers around
an open hand,

tasting the last second
before it closes.

3.

Every hour
inside the circle,
the other hand
touches
each number
shaped like a finger.

4.

The zero appears,
with no finger prints.

It is a mark of
a number
that does not heal.

5.

In the rib cage
of an open watch,

tiny wheels, a heart,
are skeletal   gears.

6.

Inside the chest

lungs click

and the face

of a clock wakes up.

From Skin to Bone

Vital sign of a patient:

check marks in boxes:

life, death. Still eyes

behind paper, film.

I touch my grandfather's

hand. Breath trembles:

silent movie. Bleach

diluted with darkness.

Eraser smudges;

it does not erase. I read

his eulogy in a crossword

puzzle. Watch black,

white television, static

shapes, the *yin* and *yang.*

A skeleton holds

the last sheet of paper

and I wait for the cursor

to stop. Today's newspaper

said, "Tomorrow's Suffering,

Yesterday's Grief." On my

page I see a checkerboard

of fill in the blanks.

I use punctuation marks

and letters to play it.

But I shiver at the clock

ticking over my shoulder

shaping itself   into a skull.

Blank Circle

Soak eyes

       in white.

Erase   ears.

Put nose

       in bleach.

Sniff   discoloring.

       Peel zero

      from   a page

             eat it.

Does it taste like styrofoam or a tooth?

Scrape   bone flakes

out of

      skull socket

to line it

      with blank   paper.

Remove   hands,

                    put in

                    envelopes.

         Drop   them

         into   the mailbox

         of   a circle.

On the Zero's Eye

Fold   the color   white.

Use it

       to polish

       the skull's   eye.

Pour   bleach

into   socket   of bone:

       see

black   strands   of hair

       surface;

       eyelashes   in milk,

       a dark   fingerprint

               on   a zero.

Skin of a Letter

Soak head in bleach.

Separate bone from skin.

Slide out the skull;

feels like   pulp.

Twist it

into   a light socket:

now look

       it is a bulb.

So when you

flick a switch

       a question mark

       should appear.

As for the white sheet

of skin.

Wring it out.

Hang over   the skeleton

       of a letter.   Let dry.

Skeleton

Take off skin;

hang in dark closet.

Do you like

how bone

sticks to skin?

Slide flesh off

so it does not slip.

Or else you

must peel your frame

out from skin.

Soak bones

in white un-

til it is milk.

Does it ache

like your tooth

in bleach?

Now dry bones.

Pour calcium in-

to a cup.

From dark closet

lift skin off

black hook.

Do not get

back into;

wrap on-

to your bones.

Square Lips

1.

     Open
the book's
       mouth.
Flip through
each   tongue:
     ink breath.

2.

Read.

Eyes with four equal sides

              are required.

3.

Stop.

     A sentence:

     a dark smile,

     and its letters:

     black teeth.

4.

Continue reading.

    But   don't

    smile back.

Or else

        the verb

        and subject

will   eat you.

Imperative

Break a sentence; use letters for teeth.

In a word missing a letter, place a tooth.

Flick a period off the page with a fingernail.

Press on the black dot; smear into a comma.

Separate a skeleton into verbs and subjects.

Until ink comes out, pinch a letter.

Use letters shaped like bones; connect a word.

In the sockets of a skull, put commas.

Push a verb to push a noun off the page.

Until it softens, rub bone against paper.

Boil the skeleton of a sentence into ink.

Suck the marrow out of a letter.

Grind up a piece of bone; make calcium ink.

For paper, soak skin in bleach.

Erase a letter until it looks like a tooth.

Amputate one letter to fix another.

Pull a punctuation mark from a sentence.

At end of sentence, remove the tiny black skull.

Crack a sentence; let the ink drain.

Dip a bone into ink; leave it to dry.

Take a bone and lay it before a verb.

Shake punctuation off the page.

Scrape the paper from a letter.

To erase a sentence, remove your tongue.

Bleach paper then put on face.

Use commas to connect bones.

Extract the ink from a sentence.

Rinse a letter in bleach; wring it out.

With the edges of paper, skin yourself;

bathe in bleach until flesh slides off;

get out and lie down like a sentence.

Images of Myself

A sentence stands up:

skeleton   slips on a period,

    trying to walk off
    the page.

Letters scatter.

    The *A*   unfolds
                into an *N.*

    The *T*   lands on
                its head
                with one leg.

    The *H*   tips over.

    The *E*   cannot get
                back up.

    The *R*   dismantles
                to *D.*

One of the O's   rolls off,

the other one   never moves.

    And other   pieces:

bones   fragments

    left over   for punctuation marks.

Bone Milk

Write the O.

Dip skull
    into bleach.

Press the letter.

Bones soften
    into calcium.

Smear a zero.

Hair dissolves
    into ink.

Erase paper.

Skin evaporates
    into foam.

Boil subject
and verb;
    condense

into liquid.

Fade   from dark,

the shade of   milk.

Suck out period.

Tooth heats

into fluid.

Now pour   skeleton

into   another skin.

Blank Skull

An i puts   a zero

over his face.

       He does not know

       his skull is

       the color of styrofoam.

He knows   under his skin

a skeleton

rubs like   paper against ink.

He finds a letter,   opens it;

shaped   like a   circle,

       it is   empty.

He likes that,

       because an O

does not blink

       if he   fills it in.

Analogy

i

On the page, a man the size of a letter

wears a white necktie and a dark suit.

j

Next to him, a woman the size of a letter, too;

she wears a white scarf and a black gown.

'

Not a punctuation sign but a mark

of accentuation written between two lovers.

ij

He says, "I am a single bone under the skin of a letter."

She says, "I too, am a letter, but I have a curved hipbone."

i-j

See them on the white bed of a page, how they hyphenate,

how they will create   language   together.

Lower Case i and j

Man

with   one leg,

        no arms,

        wears   black suit,

                white necktie.

Woman

in   black dress,

    white scarf,

           no arms too.

On   white

    sheet

both   attend

    paper   funeral;

        tears   ink.

But   you

can   put

a hyphen

between   them:

look

they are   holding hands.

i Without j

A punctuation

soaks   through

                 white.

Press   ear

         onto   blank

                 paper:

         sound   of space

         between   letters.

Dot

         without   i,

period

         without   sentence.

Let   ink

         shape

                 the hyphen

         instead of

                 a period.

Listen.

                 It will appear

                 on the page.

i Next to j

Using a white eraser

he wipes the ink off his face

and says, "I am a zero."

He does not want to look

like a dark skeleton with

with a white skull. To be

a letter means to be stuck on

paper. Instead, he will unzip

out of the black suit he wears

and throw it off the page.

Even though he still feels

detached from his body,

he will rotate his head to the left,

speak into the ear of the letter j

and say, "Why am I a letter taken

for a number when capitalized?"

i-j

Skeletons   shaped

like two

          letters.

She   holds   a comma.

He   holds   a black dot.

Each   do not   know

          the other

until   they are

laid   next to

          one another.

Underneath

          the paper

          both have   faces.

If you   look

                    under

                    the page,

you   will   see

two   lovers

shaped

like i and j

kissing   with   a hyphen.

Ars Poetica

He gave me a book and I opened it. The first line I noticed was, "The child with the blank face of an egg." Then, I felt my face erased to its skull.

There was a missing space. So I peeled off a piece of a letter from the next page. And I nudged it carefully between the i and j.

She said, "How does it feel to have your head stuck in a zero?" Silence in a moment is imagination and I replied, "It is my halo."

I erased a zero and it appeared in someone else's thoughts. The sum of a zero and zero is zero. I wrote it again; this time it made sense.

He said, "We raise it to the lips of the nearest ear." So, I began to open books, listen for ink boiling, the scent of words, coffee brewing in my ear.

I watched the clock as if reading a sentence. The numbers were letters. The short hand was a subject, the long hand, a predicate, and the seconds, a verb.

We both stared at the ceiling. I said, "My eyes feel as if they're inside cups." Then she said, "Shall I pour your eyes back into your ears?"

Language structures what we see without saying it. But I began to pull bones from sentences, and rearrange letters into skeletons.

I heard a circle as if it were a clock. It did not tick; made the sound of an insect: it was a number in the shape of a cricket.

I opened an envelope addressed to me. I pulled out a blank sheet of paper, unfolded it. In the letter: no message, no sender's name, just a white space.

"I like that you exist," she said. Like the lowercase i, my body felt present on a page: fitted in a dark suit, white necktie, and inside the black dot, a smile.

But it was the way her skin felt as she dressed into a black outfit. The way her body slipped into a long dark dress shaped like a shadow.

He picked up a stone; held it to his ear. Shook it like a broken watch. He opened it, and inside were small gears, shaped like a clock.

I am a skeleton, a sentence, too. Although like you, I am neither a meaning nor a structure, just silence in a complete thought.

Discourse

When you are naked,

                     you are unwritten.

           Put on a dark suit.   Be a letter.

Next to you,   she slips on
a black dress

              shaped like a j.

Our bodies   made of ink;   a substance

                        of *langue*.

           We only want to be written,

           to have content.

But, language likes to dress us up.
Position us

              next to one another,
so we   exist   as characters.

As someone places a hyphen

           between us,   we feel   conjunct;

it can be erased.

When it happens

        replace the blank space   with a verb,

        put a letter   *under erasure.*

Sometimes,   things written are contained;

    not in our control.

Then   we must take off   our outfits

fold them back

        remove ourselves   from the page.

Dot Fly

You will find that it lands on the letters

i and j or next to objects in sentences

to dot itself in the bone of paper

like a dark point in the center of a skull.

When you smear it, a comma appears with

its tiny dark wing; a blink will shutter

its movement into the air like a speck

of static. Catch it with your hand; bring

to your left ear and listen carefully. It sounds

like trying to connect a skull to the end

of a sentence, a headless skeleton to a tiny

round punctuation mark. It does not let the bones

or the words stumble. But whatever you do,

do not clench your hand or shake, or its wing

                will break and flap off.

Meditation

I listen to the dark zero in my skull. It sounds like ink filling a white dot on a black sheet of paper. Sometimes it is a punctuation mark with little dark wings; it does not fly, blinks like an eyelash. I always wait for the first letter to appear on the page. And when it does, it shakes its fist up at me. At times, language wants to be dressed in a suit, white necktie. But I prefer a pause between ink and letter when words are silent, unclothed. The clock on the wall swallows a fly, and I see tiny legs struggle between the teeth of a number. Somewhere inside the dark, a shadow tries to lighten the dot on the letter i. He rubs it against paper; it smears instead. This is what I like about language. The way one folds sentences and feels the bones of words, letters crack, then unfolds them, tiny dark pieces that reconnect again on the page. I do not like to go past the period, because language resists death. Because underneath, bones, subject, and verb wait to be revealed. The way one can erase milk to find calcium; the way an erased letter on the page dries into white. The top of the letter i is not *a tiny round mark made by or as if by a pointed instrument.* It can be a round letter, a blank zero, or an unwritten circle. Imagination is an equation: x and y can be added, subtracted, multiplied, and divided. *You were an unnatural birth,* she said. I was a letter in the center of an o, born and pulled out, head shaped like a punctuation mark at the sentence's end.

Quietus

The zero is not a circle; it's an empty clock. And the clock is an o which rolls to the other side of the page. But the c stuck between the b and d eats itself and the page will taste how desperate language is. If you peel a sheet of paper, you will find letters who have eaten themselves: the a who chewed itself until it became a dot on paper and the z who ingested itself until it was a tiny line on a page. Within the white spaces they have become inklings, miniature dark skulls, and black specks on paper. But they still move like the tiniest gears in a clock. And their bones are scattered like dry grains of ink on a white sheet. I think of their deaths: the stiff face of a choked letter, the broken jaw of an e, the throat of an f slit open, an i swallowed up to its torso, the dot bitten from a j, the letters of a sentence removed with teeth. A sentence dipped in bleach until it becomes a skeleton, the bones thinning into calcium, the sockets of the skull discoloring into pale ink. And you will hurt it more if you try to slip its bones back through the flesh of ink or dress it back into its dry black clothes. So let the lower case i be a body under the dot: a naked letter on the page.

Writ

A man in a black suit with a zero
for a head follows me. He carries a gun
shaped like language; wants me written
and dead on the page. He can smell
my bleach-stained letters and can taste
what I have written; the inked bones of words.
But he cannot hear me breathe. Silence
is my refuge. I see the white door of paper;
I open it and enter. I was there forever it seems,
thinking of the origin and the end of *poesis*.
I thought I had lost him somewhere between
the point and line of *language*. But he finds me,
unwritten in the depths of the page. He lifts
the barrel of his pen, center on my forehead,
pulls the trigger. Through hair, skin, bone,
I feel the weight of ink enter my forehead.
The darkness takes up the white spaces
of my skull, I let him fill me with words.

Biographical Note

Orlando White is originally from Tólíkan, Arizona. He is Diné (Navajo) of the Naaneesht'ézhi Tábaahí (Zuni Water's Edge Clan) and born for the Naakai Dinée (Mexican Clan). He holds a BFA in creative writing from the Institute of American Indian Arts and an MFA from Brown University. His poems have appeared in *Bombay Gin, In Posse Review, Oregon Literary Review, Ploughshares, They Are Flying Planes, 26 Magazine*, and elsewhere. He now lives in Santa Fe, New Mexico. *Bone Light* is his first book.

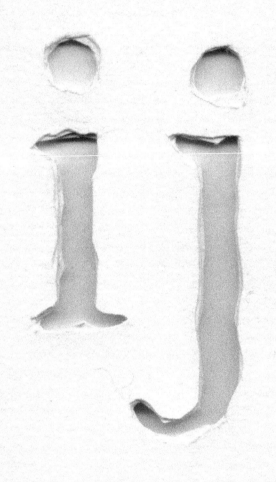